g

Jenna Baldwin

# growing up

To my grandpa

*growing up*
ISBN 978 1 76109 692 1
Copyright © text Jenna Baldwin 2023
Cover image: Georgia Nosworthy

First published 2023 by
**GINNINDERRA PRESS**
PO Box 3461 Port Adelaide 5015
www.ginninderrapress.com.au

# Contents

# Growing up

I wander up that old path and put my hand on the front door.
As I lie on their old bed I can't get the sadness from my head.
Old photos surround me as I talk in the dark.
I wonder if he can hear me.
Grandpa, I don't know what to do.
I wish I could talk to you.
The shadows dance across the room.
I feel so alone in a place I once considered home.
I don't know what has happened to me.
I can't smile.
I remember back to a summer twenty years ago.
I would lie on the blanket in the backyard.
Nanna would tell me about Sydney.
How the cicadas would sing every year.
I feel lost in my own skin.
Faces I have known for years are getting older.
I couldn't believe it when they told me he died.
I am standing on the edge of something.
I guess this is called growing up.
I close my eyes on that old bed.
I wipe the sadness from my head.
I sink so very deep as my grandpa sings me to sleep.

# The whale song

I look for him through the waves every time I walk along the beach.
A beautiful memory I just can't reach.
I search for him from the land.
I walked over those slippery rocks as they shifted beneath me.
I could hear his song.
People around me gasp with wonder and joy.
I sit next to a little boy.
As the wind blew through my hair,
I breathed in the sea air.
The water hit my cold face.
It was the sea I could taste.
He rose up from the water and his large eye looked at me.
I felt a connection sweep through me.
I fell in love with this creature from the sea.
He rolled around in the crashing waves.
Dolphins surrounded him.
The water from his blowhole touched my arm.
I climbed closer towards the sea to talk to the whale who sang to me.
The barnacles shone on his skin.
I so badly wanted to swim and touch his noble head.
I sat and watched instead.
Around me people gasped and cheered.
Then he turned his back to us and swam away.
I can't forget that magical day.
I still look for him through the ocean, waves and sea.
I hope to hear him sing to me.

## The wave

We got caught up in a wave.
Our limbs tangled together.
The water rose above our heads.
I was terrified as I hung onto you.
The sea churned around us as salt went up my nose.
I saw you sitting in the sand laughing.
Your hair was wet and stuck to your face.
Seaweed stuck between our toes.
I spat out water as I sat beside you.
The wind swept over our wet skin.
Seagulls called above us.
We don't really know each other now.
Years and time divide us.
The years we lost still make me sad,
But we were caught in a wave once and I hung onto you.

## See me

You didn't see me standing behind your deceit.
You didn't hear me speaking under your cruel words.
You didn't feel me fall apart under your cruel feet.
So you didn't see the back bone I grew.
You didn't see the flames in my eyes.
You didn't see me laugh your cruelty away.
You didn't hear me speak the truth against you.
You were so consumed with pulling me down,
You didn't see me getting up.

# Lost him

She doesn't see him at first past the billowing sheet.
When she sees the look on his face her heart begins to break.
It's a simple exchange of words that ends her world.
As she falls to her knees the neighbours hear her cry.
The world stands still in 1942.
It will always be this way for her.
As he lowers his hat and turns to walk away
The wind blows her sadness all the way to his car.
A war no one wanted.
A name written in ink.
A bullet fired aimlessly.
This is how she lost him.

# In the trenches

Thick air with nervous sweat.
Peering into the cold.
Mother said keep warm.
Donnie crouched beside me.
Best mates since six years old.
'I love ya, mate,' he whispers.
I ain't no hero.
I ain't no legend.
I'm scared.
I want this over with.
I want to feel the sun on my face.
'Anyone got a rollie?'
A man needs a smoke.
Bloody thing won't light.
Stuck to my bottom lip.
Words killing the silence.
'Over the top!'
Looking at Donnie with words caught in my throat.
'I love ya too, mate.'

# Coffee with Grandpa

It's cold and wet when I walk into the cafe.
I take my coat off and sling it over the chair.
He orders tea and I a cappuccino.
He smiles under his black beret.
He asks where the biscuits are.
I ask if he wants one and he smiles and laughs.
'No, no, no.' He waves his hand.
We talk about the same memories and laugh at the same old things.
Then I become sad as we talk about new things.
All the things I have done and people I have met
Since he's been gone.
I lean over and say,
'Grandpa, things are so weird now I don't know what to do.'
He takes my shaking hands in his big warm ones and says,
'It's okay, my little one. Everything will be all right.'
I close my eyes as tears stream down my face but I smile,
Because I am so glad he is here with me.
Then I open them and he is gone.
I am left with an empty chair.
I grab my coat and step back out into the cold but I am not alone.
I am never alone.

# Walk of shame

He walks the street he has always known towards the land of shame.
The winter wind chills his bones.
Bleeding knuckles after another fight.
He can't remember letting him go but he can remember the
sound of the door slamming in his face.
He tries to roll a cigarette but his hands won't stop shaking.
There are the same washed out faces.
People he has known all his life and some only a few weeks.
Now all the days and weeks and years roll into one.
He can't remember how old he is.
He can't remember how to smile.
It's not about thinking any more.
It's about doing whatever you can to stop.
They were the young ambitious ones.
Now they lay across the floor surrounded by pills,
Powders and bottles.
Their pain leaked out into a syringe.
He hands over the money quickly.
The cold wind lashes at his face as he steps outside.
He pulls up a sleeve to pick a scab and sees,
CALL MUM
Written in ink across his forearm.
He is suddenly filled with rage.
'I won't be back here,' he snarls,
But he knows he will.
Of course he will.

## The man he used to be

He doesn't sleep so good any more.
Hot and cold sweats.
His body won't stop aching.
Sometimes he gets up in the middle of the night,
Runs to the bathroom and leans over the toilet bowl.
She is always there ready to wipe his face.
He was a watch repairman once.
He could fix the smallest thing.
Now he can't hold his coffee mug steady.
The bench top is filled with pill bottles and containers.
All types of medications.
Sometimes he doesn't even think he is sick.
They are doing this to him.
No one can be trusted, not even her.
So he pushes her away,
But she has come too far with this man to give up now.
He sits up all night and writes long text messages.
All the things he wishes he could say.
He writes on post-it notes and sticks them all over the house
Because it feels like his thoughts, his memories, his heart
And soul are all slipping through his fingers like sand.
He doesn't know who he is any more.
He steps outside into the backyard and tries
To find something to do.
As the sun rises above him she catches a glimpse
Of the man he used to be.
He steps inside and stumbles but she holds him steady.
He looks up at her and her smile is never wavering,
But he doesn't sleep so good any more.

# Happy never afters

Don't cut through my innocence with your sharp blade.
It took me so long to see the good again.
So don't taint my drinking water with your poisoned anger.
Don't pollute my air with your cruel words.
Don't sell me your happy never afters.
Don't break my spirit with the darkness in yours.
I see the good in everyone.
I hurt all the time but I would rather see the love than feel your hate.
Don't try to fill my head with your demons because mine have left.
Don't crush my dreams because you have none of your own.
You shine bright.
Like a blood diamond.
I don't want your fears weighing me down.
I don't need your resentment because you are lost in the dark
And I found the switch.
Don't pull me to the shadows because I shine.
Don't try to break me because you are still broken.

# Paperman

She keeps him in a box in the back of her wardrobe, sealed up tight.

No matter how much he changes for her it will never be enough.

She's knocked his edges off.

Cut away the parts she doesn't like.

She's made the perfect man to love.

A man made from desperation.

A man no longer himself.

She is happy cutting his edges off,

Making him round enough to fit.

She keeps the scissors close to her heart as she pulls him apart.

I see her cut and paste the traits she hates the most.

I see him lose himself.

I see him struggle just to be.

He lets her shape his heart and make it into what she wants it to be.

As she cuts along the lines I watch him disappear.

I watch the paper fall to the floor.

She holds him in her hand, the perfect paper man.

She doesn't even see when the creases start to show

# Puppet girl

You wear that stupid smile so well.
No one could guess you were living in hell.
You'd do anything to please him.
Nothing he does could ever convince you to leave him.
You don't see what you have become.
You don't understand what he has done.
You convince yourself your life was so bad before you met him.
You tell yourself you owe him everything.
You dress the way he tells you to.
You've traded the old for the new.
Smile for the photos he takes.
Surround yourself with liars and fakes.
If you learn to do it well no one will see you fall.
No one will see you lose it all.
You hold onto his arm as he leads you through.
Your life is no longer about you.
You would do anything he tells you to.
He makes a list of all the things you do wrong.
He tells you this will one day make you strong.
He says he knows what is best for you.
You don't see him disrespect you.
You are his little play thing.
Something he doesn't have to treat right.
Someone who won't put up a fight.
All you life you have been looking for someone.
Someone to save you when you start to sink.
Someone to tell you what to do so you don't have to think.
He pulls your puppet string so well.

He does what he wants because he knows you won't tell.
Blink those dumb eyes and tell the same lies.
Just know everything has a price when someone else
Controls the roll of your dice.
You will never be the person I once knew.
Now I know what happened to you.
I see you fall into his arms.
You wear the mask so well.
No one could guess you were destined for hell.

# Keeping in the lines

You were so good at keeping in the lines.
Your hand so steady as you guided mine.
You seemed so lost all the time.
Your mouth would smile but not your eyes.
A child sees through the lies.
So gentle your actions and so soft your words.
You would sit outside and watch the birds.
You taught me to colour in.
To use purple and green and mix it all in.
I loved you in my childlike way.
I would hang on every word you'd say.
I didn't understand when they told me you'd died.
What was suicide?
I watched them as they held each other and cried.
A darkness began to follow me.
As I got older that darkness grew.
I found you at the cemetery not long ago.
I told you how I remember your hands
Guiding my small ones along.
I know that darkness I felt was wrong.
You taught me what gets left behind.
You left it there for me to find.
I buy colouring books and when I feel it's something I want to do,
I open them and I colour in with you.

# The beast in him

In the morning it is mainly still.
It doesn't make a sound.
It smiles behind his eyes.
It's a lonely life even surrounded by others.
He can never outrun it,
The beast in him.
It wears his clothes.
It drives his car.
It tells it's stories to hopeful eyes.
It's never far behind.
It plays the part so well.
Sometimes he nearly forgets it's there.
One foot in front of the other your shadow is always there.
All his lies sound pretty coming from it's mouth.
It's been there from the start sharpening its claws.
It will be there until the very end curled around his heart.
Sometimes he just forgets as he smiles with its mouth.

# His sketch

When they told him his mind went blank as he looked at her face.
He thought it odd that even though everything in his life
Had just changed, her face remained the same.
So he made sure to take in every small detail
From her long hair to her small ankles.
So when the time comes for them to tell him the worst part
He will be able to close his eyes,
And see her instead of this long, dark tunnel.
He wants to see something beautiful.
So he sketches her in his mind.
The perfect replica.
When the bad times come and the sad words are spoken
And even through everything will change again,
He can take solace in the fact that she never will.

## The best and worst

The house was always dirty.
We didn't eat much.
Alcohol fuelled our need for anything else.
The music was always up loud.
As we talked, fought and yelled the three of us,
Just getting through.
We were in and out of pubs, parties and people's cars.
I forgot all the things I once found so important.
We stole stupid things and slept on mattresses on the floor.
We slept to the sound of each other's breathing.
We marched to the beat of our own drums.
We were young and we were free.
So it went on and on.
It was the worst and best time of my life.

# The edge

We wasted our time and our youth on each other,
But I loved getting wasted with you.
I held the back of your coat as you led me through.
Bottle of wine in your hand as I spilled bourbon down my shirt.
The music was loud as we screamed to talk.
I felt safe with you.
Your house was like Andy Warhol's factory.
All the misfits together.
I felt at home with you.
I think I loved you.
Sisters but not by blood.
Our souls matched and I liked that you never laughed
At the silly things I said.
We were mentally ill with alcohol as medicine.
I didn't realise until I found you on the floor.
Your limp hand held mine all the way to the hospital.
My heart always broke with yours.
I always talked too loud, loved too hard and cared too much,
But I got better,
And you…
Well, you didn't.
We were always at the very edge but I always felt
It was the best place to be until I lost you.
Your cruel words echo back at me.
I grieved for you even though you were still alive.
We danced together when the boys were afraid of us.
I held your hand when you were afraid of yourself.
You aren't in my life any more and it hurts that you will never
know how much I miss you.
Because when I was afraid I was getting too close to the edge.
You always told me I could fly.

# Letting go

'It's okay, Dad, you can let go now.'
I told you as I sat upon my new bike.
Your apprehensive hands finally let me go
As I sailed away from you.
I was afraid at first but I could hear you cheering me on.
I pedalled faster.
Soon you became a small figure in the distance.
I see you now as the pain controls your life.
Your disease controls your soul.
Your wary smile makes me crumble inside.
I just want to hold you.
I want to tell you softly,
Even though I am afraid,
'It's okay, Dad. You can let go now.'

# Who you used to be

I can't remember the exact moment I lost you.
When you let go of my hand.
I don't recall watching you step into the darkness,
Or when I finally let go of the idea I had of you in my head.
But I remember sitting with you and laughing so much
Our stomachs hurt.
I remember sunny, drunk days with you.
My head in your lap.
We walked side by side and you held my bags for me.
I remember the sound of your laugh and the smell of you.
When I called you my best friend.
When I called you my brother.
I don't remember when you first started using.
Or when your clothes started to hang off you.
When you stopped answering my calls.
When I started to fear for you,
But I remember eating sticky ice creams in bed with you.
How we sang to music as we lay on our backs in the grass.
We swam in summer and hit each other with wet towels.
The shadows never reached us.
I thought we would be friends forever.
Your heart was the same as mine.
I don't remember when you first lost your spark.
When I couldn't see the boy in your eyes an ymore.
But I remember when you made me laugh.
How your arms held me tight.
When I thought we were invisible.

See, I don't remember how or why you changed.
All I can remember is how you used to be.
It replays in my head over and over,
And that,
That is what's killing me.

# The ones I can't reach

Why do I miss the ones I can't reach?
Old photos dog-eared from touch.
I carry memories like precious stones,
Hanging heavily around my neck.
Why do I cry for what is lost?
Old faces haunt me.
Stumbling in corridors empty and cold.
I am alone at every party.
Why can't I be content with what I have?
My feet never touch the floor.
Why do I hold on when it's easier to let go?
It still hurts when I hear your name.
Old friends and lovers never really leave my life.
Their ghosts make a home in my heart.
So many people inside it is easy to be torn apart.
Why do I do the same sad dance when I know
How the night will end?
Constantly reaching out for hands who have long since
Let go of mine.
Every rejection and unanswered question buried in my soul.
I am learning to let go a little day by day.
With every person I let go my heart still doesn't feel the same.
Love runs deep in these bones.
Pain was just a part of the deal.
Now I know why I miss the ones I can't reach.
Endless nights of no sleep.
Tears that flowed out of me.
Always looking for the ones who left.
I was too blind to see the ones who stayed.

# Granite Island

You always walked ahead of me but the wind carried your voice.
Fishing rods over our shoulders and bourbon in my bag.
The nights we sat side by side.
Laughing at the world.
When your arm rested next to mine.
We would look at the stars.
The ocean would sing to us.
I would crack open a can as our rods sat side by side.
As I sat with you,
Moonlight shining down,
I wondered if life could get any better than this?

# Stingray

I know I have invaded your home.
Large feet in the sand.
Your curious little eyes watch me.
You swim around my feet.
You glide through the water.
We mean each other no harm, you and I.
Your are beautiful as you swim beside me.
Your presence astounds me.
I am so grateful you have shared your home with me.

# Another one down

He crouched low in the mud.

Eye closed as if to block out the thud.

The bodies slip past his fingers.

Death still lingers.

Eighteen years old is too young to be this close to the end.

To watch the death of another friend.

Salt water to his thighs and then he heard her call to him.

He never believed in mermaids until she called his name.

Things will never be the same.

He walked deeper still.

The water lapped at his hips.

As he reaches out for her hand, her kind eyes seemed to understand.

Her hair so soft against his face.

Her beauty took him away from this place.

All around him a war went on but with his mermaid he was gone.

Bullets rained down as he kissed her lips.

Her wet hands on his hips.

Screams could no longer reach his ears.

She chased away all his fears.

It is so cold now as he closed his eyes.

Blood spread through the water as she held him in her arms.

Her lips still on his face.

Salt water he could taste.

As the darkness crept on he felt himself go.

It was so quiet and peaceful then.

He couldn't hear a sound.

The mermaid takes another one down.

# Jase 1

He was lost in darkness for so long.
It became normal.
A needle in his arm became normal,
And all the parties and all the drugs became his life.
He bowed down to temptation.
He was lost for so long.
He never looked for a different path.
Somehow, somewhere,
Some light got through.
Day by day and piece by piece he began to walk away
From the dark.
He stumbled a lot.
The pain of learning to live again.
He never gave up on that light.
Now the dark is gone.
The sun touches his face.
The light found my friend and so did I.

# Waiting

You were gone for so long.
Your absence I got used to.
The hole you left never really healed.
I got used to the pain it left.
I looked for you.
I looked for so long.
I could never find you in the dark.
And you never answered when I called your name.
So in time I stopped looking for you.
Though it broke my heart.
I got used to missing you.
Then one day sitting alone a shadow fell over me.
You were gone for so long.
I never thought you'd be back.
As your shadow melts into mine I feel you beside me.
It never occurred to me through all the searching and all the pain,
All I needed to do was wait for you to come back.

## The worst part

I know you have been gone for years now.
I have grown used to life without you.
Then I get that smell.
The smell of you.
All of a sudden you are here again if only for a moment.
I am wrapping my arms around you.
I can almost feel you.
Then I remember that you are gone,
And my heart breaks all over again.

# Uninvited guest

Loneliness comes crashing in like an old friend
I haven't seen in months,
Smashing and breaking things in its path.
Smothering my heart until all can see,
Are all the things I don't have.

## Locket

The days I spent with you,
The years laced up in a perfect little locket.
I carry you with me always.

# Dave

I hear his voice say my name before I reach the front door.
I cannot control the smile that crosses my face.
Old friends we are and you can tell by the way
We address each other.
Years mean nothing when the connection is strong.
It has been a few years since I have seen him.
My old friend offers me a cup of tea.
He still makes me laugh just the way he used to.
Hearts that have never parted.
The time we spent apart doesn't mean a thing.
Our hearts could never let go.
You always hold onto the important ones.

# Men don't talk about their feelings

'Men don't talk about their feelings,' Hew told me
As I put my hand on his shoulder.
My grandpa never did.
He kept his secrets inside.
He kept the cancer a secret until it ate him alive.
Why do they tell us tears are weakness when it takes guts
To let it out?
It takes balls to be vulnerable.
Why do they tell us feelings should be private?
Locked away in our hearts and souls.
So much hidden behind a smile.
So much pressure in a locked-up heart.
He didn't think he could talk to anyone.
In a society that tells us mental illness is a weakness
And men do not cry.
So he kept it locked in his own secret heart.
Day by day it sat there, poisoning his soul.
You could have talked to me.
You could have reached out to me.
I would have held you.
They found his body not far from home.
His skin was still warm when she touched his hand.
She lost him that day under the morning sun as the birds sang.
He did the only thing he could do,
Because men don't talk about their feelings.

# The bullet

When I was little my grandpa would point to the small scar
Above his eyebrow and say,
'That is where the bullet went in, in the war
And came out the other side.'
I would look at him in wonder.
For years I believed him.
Then as I got older I would roll my eyes and say,
'Grandpa, I know you got that scar from falling
Onto the iron bedhead when you were little.'
But now,
Now I would give just about anything to hear that story again.

# It's quiet now

It's quiet now.
The rattle in your chest has stopped.
Your body is so still.
I hold your hand until your skin grows cold.
I feel you slip away.
Somewhere I can't go.
I call your name in an empty house.
I hold my chest to stop the sobs.
In your old room I can still smell you.
It's quiet now.
No more roar from your motorbike.
The hands that once held drumsticks and fixed watches
Are still now.
They are quiet now.
I will never hear your laugh again.
It's so quiet now.
I know your pain is over.
Peace touches your soul,
But you've left me with this silence.
This silence I can't control.
The house is so quiet,
But what I feel inside my heart,
Inside the hole you left,
Is so very loud.

# Grief

Grief never really leaves you.
It's a constant passenger in your car.
The box you try to keep closed.
Hands tight around the wheel as your tears blind you.
It's the knife you wish you could use to cut out
Your own aching heart.
The life you would give just so they could live again.
I can't stop seeing your face in my head.
Grief is my new best friend,
And it's set up home in my head.
All the people I have lost are there with you.
It is so hard to live with ghosts when you are still alive.
My smile isn't fooling anyone.
Grief never really leaves you.
The box just gets easier to close.
You'll never leave me.
Grief comes with anger.
The screams I scream.
Sadness comes with nothingness.
I want to be with you.
I want it all to stop,
But my love for you is greater than that.
We learn to live with grief.
The constant passenger,
Until one day smiles replace the tears.
The ache becomes sweet,
And I smile when I hear you name.

# One more day

I don't know what to do.
My heart aches when I think about you.
I would give anything to once again be by your side.
Sharing a joke and smiling at something you've said.
Sitting in your lounge room with a coffee in my hand.
I wish I could have had just one more day with you.
Standing at your front door,
But you aren't there.
Not any more.
I wish I could have one last hug from you.
One last Op Shop trip.
You always laughed when I put silly hats on my head.
One last coffee date with you.
We would make up silly stories about everyone who walked by.
You always had time for me.
Where did that time go?
It escaped when I wasn't looking.
Now more than anything I want more.
I wish,
Oh, how I wish,
I could have just one more day with you.

## Jase 2

Now things are more dull.
There is less sparkle.
There is less glitter in the sir.
The world went a little darker,
When your light went out.

# Jack

I love to hold his little face in my hands.
To feel his heart beat next to mine.
I die when he smiles at me.
I melt when he laughs.
He makes all the darkness go away.
He is sunshine and light.
They say we take care of our children.
I wonder if they will ever know how much they take care of us.

## You make me smile

You make me smile when you smile.
Your little eyes light up.
My heart melts when your small fingers curl through mine.
You make me smile when I don't feel like it.
Your beautiful face lights up the dark.
You make me laugh when you laugh.
When you are a little boy running around the schoolyard,
When you are a solemn teen sitting in your room,
Even when you are a man with maybe a family of your own,
You will always make me smile when you smile.

# Unicorns

Her co-workers make fun of her.
The fifty-year-old woman with pink unicorns on her desk.
They snigger at her dangly white unicorn earrings
That catch the light.
They laugh at her unicorn mug.
People are surprised at the unicorns adorning her lounge room.
Glittering eyes and shining manes.
They don't see the large pink unicorn on her dressing table.
The one above the small framed photo of a happy little girl.
A little girl who called her Mummy.
A little girl who has been missing nearly twenty years now.
A little girl who loved unicorns.

# What Nanna taught me

She had green eyes that were always smiling.
She wore odd socks and bright clothes.
Nothing matched.
She carried herself with the freedom of not caring
What other people thought.
Her house was filled with odd and ends.
Random pictures she liked from magazines taped to her walls.
She would stop and talk to anyone who looked sad.
She didn't see age or race or anything else.
All she saw was a potential friend.
She walked with sunshine in her heart.
She taught me the best way to live life is to live free.
To have the freedom to be yourself.

# Rooms

There are many rooms in my heart.
Many with people inside, stumbling around and making a mess.
There is an empty room.
Sometimes it hurts me to think of it.
It gives me a sad, lonely ache.
It's the only room I keep locked.
It's where you used to be.

# Sweetheart

I feel his little arms hold me tight.
Soft hair against my face.
Warm little body against my own.
My love fills the need for anything else,
But the sound of his sweet little heart.

# The last goodbye

I touched his hand when it was still warm.
I bent down to kiss his sleeping head.
I said,
'I love you, Dad. I will see you tomorrow.'
But sometimes tomorrow never comes.
I said,
'I love you, Dad.'
And he was gone.

# The lost boys

a poem for the victims of Jeffery Dahmer

His mother didn't know how to love him.
His father loved him enough to stay away.
The loneliness started early.
Like a disease.
Couldn't relate to other people.
He felt like he was watching them underwater.
When everyone leaves you how do you make just one stay?
Once they were cold and the life left their bones
He could hold them.
Hands gripping dead skin.
Please don't leave me.
Please don't leave.
They are all lost boys now.
Faded photos in a book.
He was only fourteen.
Oh god, he was only fourteen.
Their mothers wept for them.
Candles lit for sons never coming home.
Their mothers tore themselves apart.
Please don't leave me.
Please don't leave.
His mother never held him when he was a boy.
His father ignored the warning signs flashing in his eyes.
He found a way to keep them.
Now they can never leave.
They will never grow up.
Life taken from their bones.
All the ones who never got to go home.

His darkness ate everything in its path.
A mother still lights a candle.
It shines through the dark.
There is nothing worse than feeling alone.
One day they will all come home.

# BPD Survivor

(borderline personality disorder)

Hey there, it's been a few days.
Looks like you are back again.
You are the dark thing curled around my heart.
You have been there from the start.
Behind my smile.
Behind my shaking hands.
You are holding the reins again.
I know they don't understand because you make me
So happy and bubbly then.
Making me feel like I am on top of the world.
This is the best day of my life.
It hurts more the higher you fall.
You whisper to me in the dark,
'Your friends don't really like you. Everyone hates you.
Your son would be better off without you.'
Mocking words and sharp teeth but soon it's okay again.
I love everything so much my heart might burst.
Here is my heart on my sleeve.
That is why I die every time they leave.
Please don't leave me.
No, get away from me.
I can't contain the feelings inside me.
Look in the mirror who am I meant to be?
Little voice is talking to me.
'You will never amount to anything.
Know how to stop the hurt in your head?
The pain goes away once you're dead.'
Stop these feelings.

I would give anything to stop the emotions flooding out of me.
I understand their pain.
I understand too much.
Faded scars on my wrist.
Tiered eyes look back at me.
Can't sleep again.
Brain is playing back every cruel word ever said to me.
Lie awake in the dark.
I hold onto what is left of my heart.
Sorry I talk too much.
Sorry I hold on too tight.
I just can't bare the thought of losing you.
Nails digging into skin.
No, I won't let it win.
I will fight this day after day.
I will fight the cruel things you say.
Scars on my hands and wounds on my heart.
I have been this way from the very start.

# Large popcorn

I want to see the light through the dark,
But I am not afraid to walk alone at night in the park.
I want to drink these bad feelings away.
I want to mean what I say.
I think I'm going to sit in the dark and watch a movie.
I am going to sit in the cinema in the dark and dream for a while.
I will put my feet up in the aisle.
I am going to watch these people with the happy, smiling faces.
Their picket white fences.
I will pretend my life is as wonderful as theirs.
I think I am going to just dream for a while.
They say nothing is ever easy and nothing comes for free.
Things have gotten far too hard for me.
They say the one you love is always worth the fight.
What if you end up alone crying every night?
I thought I knew what I wanted but I was fooling myself.
All these bourbons aren't good for my health.
I guess when you smile, laugh and act dumb.
You can fool anyone.
Lately things have gotten too real.
I pick at the scab so it will never heal.
I just want to get lost for a while.
People always tell me things I don't want to hear.
Alcohol stops the fear.
I am going to chill with my Pepsi and large popcorn.
I will laugh and smile in all the right parts.
I am going to be like those happy people with the unbroken hearts.
I don't need friends who are never around.
I don't need another drink before I hit the ground.

Sometimes people secretly hate you
When you tell them you are doing okay.
I have had the worst fucking day.
So I am going to sit in the back and laugh and smile.
I am going to get lost in someone else's life for a while.

# Heartbreak education

They don't teach you the important stuff in school.
They don't teach you about heartache.
About a pain so imense you want to rip yourself apart.
They don't teach you the nature of the human heart.
I wish I had a heartbreak education that taught me
How to deal with this.
I never needed algebra or history.
I just want to know what is happening to me.
What is this awful sadness that brings me to my knees?
What is this terrible anger that makes me scream these things?
Why can't I sleep at night?
Teacher, I am really not all right.
I feel like I am falling apart.
I don't understand my own heart.
Why do people lie?
Why do I lie awake at night and cry?
What really makes a good lover?
All these things I don't understand.
I know I am too old to have someone hold my hand.
But I just want to stop this ache.
I want to heal myself before I break.
No one ever teaches you these things.
No one teaches you how to cope with life.
You just have to fight your way through.
You get no heartbreak education,
It's all up to you.
When I happens you have to find the right thing to do.
I am hurting now and it makes no sense.
I would rather feel thean be numb.
Heartbreak happens to everyone.

I don't feel good today.
It maybe a long time before I am okay.
I know what to do.
I am going to fight my way through.

# Black lace and sad eyes

Things seem so better when you are drunk.
When you are so happy you don't realise your ship has sunk.
Things are so much better when someone touches you
In all those special places.
Nothing ever happens like you want it to.
It's made you so cruel.
Older men like black lace and sad eyes.
A silly smile to hide the lies.
If I could retrace my steps and find you there,
You still wouldn't care.
He would hold you and remind you how to breathe.
He could remind you how to love.
He doesn't love you either.
Doesn't it make you shiver?
The years go by so quick and there isn't enough eyeliner
To hide the truth.
You wish you could bottle the sadness of your youth,
And carry it close to your heart.
Things looks so much better when you are on all fours
As he holds your hips.
You have such soft lips,
But he will never touch them like you want him to.
When you walk home alone.
You dread your empty home.
So you sit by the sea.
You let the wind caress your skin.
You let the water wash away your sin.
You fall into the sand.
You are drunk and your ship has just sunk.

In the darkness of the night you are such a beautiful sight.
On the sand with eye open wide,
Waiting for the oncoming tide.

# Stay

The streets are wet.
The air is damp.
I see you through the flickering lamp.
Your eyes are sad and your mouth twisted.
Tears fall down your cheeks.
You rest your head on my shoulder.
We are different now that we are older.
Your words are slurred, sad and tangled.
The bottle rests at your feet.
We share body heat.
You bury your face in my arms.
I hold you close.
I worry for you the most.
Your body is slack in my arms.
Your hair smells nice.
Like all the things from the past I love.
The wind is cold.
As others talk and laugh I whisper to you words of comfort.
You think you are alone.
To me you and your house were always home.
Our boots sit side by side.
To you I am tied.
Your make up is all smudged and your pretty face looks away.
It is all coming out today.
You speak of your dreams, hopes and fears.
I try my best to catch all your tears.
The river is our special place.
Here you show me your saddest face.
I wish I could give you something real to feel.

Something to hold onto,
But all I can give is me,
And all the good in you I see.
Do you remember that sunny day we lay on the grass laughing?
I think that was the last time I was happy.
I wish you would dance with me.
I don't know what to say on this cold dark day.
I wish I could find the words to say,
Please stay,
Don't go away.
The streets are wet.
The air is damp.
I turn off my bedside lamp.
I think of you and how much you mean to me,
And how I wish I could make you see.

# The boy in the sky

for Kris

'Did you hear about Kris?'
He looked at me as his hands shook.
'He died.'
I stumbled onto the bench,
Eyes filled with tears.
My mind filled with memories of the happy,
Colourful boy with green eyes.
The colours of his bright Hawaiian shirts captivating me.
His friendly grin as he led me through school.
My sweet friend.
Tears still come as I looked up at the sky.
I could still see him in the bright colours of the sky.
I see him in the swirls of red, orange and pink.
Smiling.
Waving to me.

# Josh

I look up to see his smiling face.
Lighting up the place.
We embrace in a hug.
He walks with the same jump in his step.
The same sparkle in his eyes.
My happy, silly friend.
We laugh at the same silly things.
He smiles at all my jokes.
My old friend still gets me.
As we grow we lose friends.
Parts of us drift away.
The good ones stay.
We throw balls at each other and run through the store laughing.
Sometimes things don't stay the same.
Life can be strange.
Then there are people like him who don't change at all.
His light makes me feel warm inside.

# I am not afraid

The water is cold around my middle but the heat
Has not escaped my body.
Not until it starts to rain.
Thunder booms in the distance.
It's dangerous to be here.
Wading through the waves.
I am not scared as the rain stings my face.
I stick out my tongue.
The waves churn around me.
Lighting splashes across the sky.
It strikes beneath the water.
I look up at the sky as I stretch my arms out beneath the water.
I lift my head.
I hear the thunder roar.
I am not afraid.

# Ghosts

Sometimes when it is quiet I hold my broom steady.
I look up at the stairs.
These two girls come running down.
One with black hair loose as her boots thump down.
The other in baggy jeans and a jumper.
They seem so close.
Their shoulders touch.
Their dreams are still real and unbroken.
Then slowly they fade away.
And I am unable to tell you I saw our ghosts today.

# Old days

They tell me you still talk about the old days.
Limp cigarette hanging from your hand.
I wonder if you still carry that cask with you everywhere you go.
I don't know if I can forgive.
If I can let go.
Time has made me wiser.
Time has made me colder.
You never said you were sorry.
I guess that is what hurts the most.
You never said you were wrong.
Sometimes I wonder if I could ever really let you go.
Because they tell me you still smile
When you talk about the old days.

# The hardest goodbye

There is a ghost inside her head.
A cold empty spot in her bed.
There is an unanswered question on her mind.
There is an answer she will never find.
She wishes she could see you smile one last time.
It's driving her out of her mind.
There is a mother crying for her son.
Cursing the darkness.
The darkness that won.
There are your mates crying on each other's shoulders.
Why couldn't they see it in your eyes?
You got so good at telling lies.
There is a sadness in this town.
Your absence drags them down.
When there is no answer and no one knows why.
It's the hardest goodbye.
Teachers remember you as a happy little boy.
You would always share your toy.
You were the one making everyone else happy.
The Joker with the broken heart.
It tears your family apart.
How can they go on without you?
You are there in every joke.
In every photo they ever took.
You are there in your child's eyes.
Sometimes people give up the fight.
It doesn't mean they are out of our sight.
Only you know the reason why.
For you this was the hardest goodbye.

# A soldier's love

A name etched in stone.
A photo covered in dust and stood alone.
My great-grandpa's name on that memorial stone.
My grandpa went to war too.
Lied about his age at seventeen.
He never told me about the things he had seen.
I have a photo of him.
So young and full of promise.
A small town boy on a big adventure.
He packed as quick as he could.
In those hopeful eyes there was a spark.
Sometimes he would lie awake in the dark.
They sold him so many half truths.
They didn't tell him about the fear.
Of overcoming pain and heartache every year.
Losing you best friends.
Watching them fall into the mud.
Jumping at the sound of every thud.
Carrying heavy rifles makes you arms so sore.
Sitting in the rain with clothes ripped and tore.
He never really spoke of the darkness of the war.
Instead he told me about her.
Hanging out waiting to be drafted home.
When he wasn't drinking he was sitting alone.
That is when this country boy met the pretty city girl.
When she kissed him all the darkness went away.
She knew he couldn't stay.
So she risked it all and moved to a small town.
Away from the city they couldn't hear a sound.

They loved each other for more than fifty years,
It was the war that brought them together.
And they braved all the bad weather,
Holding hands.
That is what I think of on ANZAC day.
A love story that overpowered the pain.
A pretty girl who made my grandpa live again.

# Birthday blues

You were drunk at my birthday.
Your voice raised above everyone else's.
Your hair hanging in your face.
Your hollow accusations.
Your hostile sneer.
Why did I think things would be different?
You sit down and take another swig from the bottle.
There are no apologies here for us.
I watch you walk away as I look at my melted birthday cake.
Candles sliding to the side.
They were always saying bad things about you.
And for the first time in years I finally believe them.

# Why he wouldn't come

When I was small I would wonder why he wouldn't come.
His hands holding the newspaper steady.
I'd want to run towards the crashing waves of the sea
But his eyes would look down to the floor.
I did not know what those eyes would see in that deep blue sea.
He was a young man then,
When he dragged the bodies from the sea.
He was just a kid when he gently closed their dead eyes.
Where I saw fun and happiness all he could see was death.
He never really talked about it,
The war.
I wish I had known back then.
I would have held his shaking hands.
I think he thought he was weak.
But I always thought of him as the strongest man
I have ever known.